FLEURISH

Fleurish

PHOTOGRAPHY BY ILONA

TEXT BY VERONICA D'ORAZIO

SASQUATCH BOOKS
SEATTLE

Printed in China
Published by Sasquatch Books
Distributed by Publishers Group West
12 11 10 09 08 07 06 05   6 5 4 3 2 1

Photography: Ilona
Book design: Stewart A. Williams

Library of Congress Cataloging-in-Publication Data
Ilona.
        Fleurish / photographs by Ilona ; text by Veronica D'Orazio.
        p. cm.
        ISBN 1-57061-438-5
        1. Flowers—Pictorial works. 2. Flowers. 3. Photography of plants. I. D'Orazio, Veronica. II. Title.

SB407.I57 2005
635.9'022'2—dc22
                                                              ·
                                                       2004051082

Sasquatch Books / 119 South Main Street, Suite 400 / Seattle, WA 98104 / (206) 467-4300
www.sasquatchbooks.com / custserv@sasquatchbooks.com

To Sheila, the best sister ever. I love you.

ACKNOWLEDGMENTS
Thanks to Veronica D'Orazio, for your beautiful words and spirit. Gary Luke, for your vision and passion for this project, and for saying yes and no. The hard-working team at Sasquatch Books, I am honored.
To my sons Landon and Leif, who would rather see more BMX bikes and skateboards, but know a mom is also a person.

To Lenny, for the wonderful hikes among the wildflowers. Thanks to my Mom, Christa, for being the great mom you are. My friend Christa Langhammer, for giving me, and my cameras, a safe place away from home; your friendship is a gift.

To the two women who really started it all for me: Oma, who left a very big impact, guiding my small hands through the wonders of European flower markets. And Grandma, who taught me all about sweet peas and forget-me-nots. My family and friends, you are the flowers in life.

"The flower is the poetry of reproduction.

It is an example of the eternal seductiveness of life."

Jean Giraudoux

There are days we live as if death were nowhere in the background: from joy to joy to joy, from wing to wing, from blossom to blossom to impossible blossom, to sweet impossible blossom."

Li-Young Lee

left: Daisy *Osteospermum*

Waves of light travel from sun to flower. The flower receives all the colors in the visible spectrum, absorbs them into itself, and then reflects back the color it chooses for us to see. And we see so much. For every color in the floral spectrum, there are infinite combinations of hue and tone, endless gradations of light and dark. A bearded iris may look lavender in early

left: Camellia *Camellia japonica*

morning and by afternoon becomes a moody mauve. Hydrangeas can change colors several times over the course of their life cycle, beginning celadon green, for example, then spilling over in time into rich, tone-on-tone hues of amethyst and maroon, lilac and root beer. When we look closely at a flower, the eye moves through texture and shape to get closer to the

right: Gardenia *Gardenia*

reddest red, the most saturated violet, the palest, softest green. The colors a flower reflects take us deeper into our own psychology, where the blossoms encompass our deepest human longings.

left: Alpine Violet *Cyclamen*

top: Hydrangea *Hydrangea macrophylla* **right:** Moth Orchid *Phalaenopsis*

Camellia *Camellia*

Oriental Lily *Lilium*

left: Mexican Aster *Cosmos* **top:** Magnolia *Magnolia grandiflora*

top: Gerbera Daisy *Gerbera* **right:** Dahlia *Dahlia*

An abiding impulse exists just under the surface of our endless exploration of flowers: we need their wildness. Quietly, assuredly, their beauty disrupts the field of time. The floral kingdom precedes us. It will outlive us. When we truly see a flower, we give ourselves over to the moment. Without even trying, we trust the flower's loveliness and enter its world: an

left: Tulip *Tulipa*

immensely generative, fecund world that buzzes and hums with life, that gives succor, entices, inspires. We are drawn to the silent serenity of dove-white magnolia blossoms, a hushed whiteness: innocent, sacrosanct, the pollen resting on their petals like a kind of pious offering.

right: Daisy *Leucanthemum maximum*

left: Calla Lily *Zantedeschia* **top:** Chrysanthemum *Chrysanthemum*

left: Hellebore *Helleborus* **top:** Coneflower *Rudbeckia*

left: Anthurium *Anthurium* **top:** Gladiola *Gladiolus*

Hellebore *Helleborus*

Oxalis *Oxalis*

left: Poppy *Papaver rhoeas* **top:** Lupine *Lupinus*

Feeling less than virtuous, we may peek under the shirred petticoats of ranunculus, where lime green stems seep their greenness into the beginning pinks and whites of their ruffled petals. From there the eye is drawn upward and inward toward the round, generous whorl of layer

left: Orchid *Phalaenopsis*

upon layer of petals. Shocking, the sheer, dense excess of the ranunculus bloom: petitely packed, indulgence without guilt. Sunflowers remind us to be playful. Happy with height, waving to us from the roadside, impossibly yellow, their fringy

petals frame their faces like baby bonnets.
Climbing roses insist on being touched.
Signaling their intent in every color
imaginable, they cast their wide nets and
wait. Pure sexual energy, all want and
need: they own their desire.

left: Golden Trumpet Tree *Tabebuia*

left: Daffodil *Narcissus* **top:** Ranunculus *Ranunculus*

top: Orchid *Cymbidium* **right:** Rosa *Rosa*

top: Sunflower *Helianthus* **right:** Tête-à-tête Narcissus *Narcissus*

overleaf: Sunflower *Helianthus* **left:** Gerbera Daisy *Gerbera* **top:** Zinnia *Zinnia*

Certainly flowers are the finest flirts, courting insects and birds with intoxicating scents, dizzying colors. Experts at mimicry, orchids can have even the most hesitant wasp newly convinced he has found his soulmate, this flower that *looks* and *smells* like his one true love, but yet resists him outright. Tripping backward over himself, he stumbles into the void of

left: Sunflower *Helianthus*

silken dust and expert curves. He vibrates
with need, tries again and again to fly off
with his sweetheart, to mate in air above
the world—so romantic!—but leaves
instead, dejected, an unwitting pollinator,
carrying her load of pollen on his back to

Sunflower *Helianthus*

fertilize the next flower he falls for. Other
insects will serve time in the penal folds of
certain flowers just to get a taste of them,
sometimes passing an entire night in the
loveliest of jail cells, until, pollination
complete, their captors open like eyes to
the morning and set their jailbirds free.

left: Sunflower *Helianthus*

Poppy *Papaver*

Freesia *Freesia*

left: Dahlia *Dahlia* **top:** Orchid *Orchid*

top: Clivia *Clivia* **right:** Begonia *Begonia*

Flowering Maple *Abutilon megapotamicum*

Blood Lily *Scadoxus*

For insects, it is largely the scent that draws them to the bloom. For birds, it is the color. For us, it is both. It is everything. Winter sunlight on white camellias. The powdery smell of wisteria in April, the vine itself Hellenic in its beauty. The kempt composure of calla lilies, and yet their

left: California Poppy *Eschscholzia californica*

yellow spathes so unabashedly erect.
Cosmos that smell like chocolate—the
entire universe contained in their rich, dark
scent. The way tulips lean and stretch
away from their vase: curving, curious. We
swoon over endless rows of yellow tulips

and marvel over the one lone red bloom cropping up out of nowhere amidst its brethren. What bravery! We could all learn from such self-possession.

left: Calla Lily *Zantedeschia* **top:** Blood-Red Trumpet Vine *Distictis buccinatoria*

top: Alpine Violet *Cyclamen* **right:** Angel's Trumpet *Brugmansia*

overleaf: Alpine Violet *Cyclamen* **top:** Orchid *Paphiopedilum* **right:** Camellia *Camellia*

left: Hibiscus *Hibiscus* **top:** Spider Flower *Cleome*

And what of the black tulips, a variety named Queen of the Night? Their color must be one of the most elusive of the flower world's offerings. Dark like a birthmark, dusky-edged. Too dark to be aubergine, and yet not quite the oblivion of absolute blackness. The plum petals

left: Water Lily *Nymphaea*

cleave the pistil, the pistil fuzzy with pollen, and the stamen: so poised to spring forth and secure every moment. Around the stamen, a dark circular band accentuates them. A circle the color of hematite, of gunmetal, shot through with indigo. And yet, still, the color of Queen of the Night:

right: English Daisy *Bellis perennis*

how to describe this? It changes every time the sunlight shifts. Most mercurial in her royal finery, she commands the play of light and shade.

left: Crabapple *Malus*

left: Pansy *Viola* **top:** Camellia *Camellia*

Rockrose *Cistus*

Dahlia *Dahlia*

overleaf: Dahlia *Dahlia* **left:** Aster *Aster* **top:** Hollyhock *Alcea*

Opium poppies are perhaps the most frowsy of flowers, crenulated, dyeing their crimson petals inky black, their petals blown open, lasciviously red. They are not unlike naughty girls who stumble home past curfew, tipsy with kisses and liquor, their short skirts outrageous, mascara

left: Dahlia *Dahlia*

staining their lusty cheeks. And at the opposite extreme: dahlias. These are the glamorous starlets, so ostentatiously dressed—and yet so well put together.

When they grow old they age discreetly
from the back of the bloom, near the base
of their stems, their petals withering for
days out of view before they fade away
completely, dignified till the end.

left: Rose *Rosa*

Oriental Poppy *Papaver orientale*

Salvia *Salvia*

top: Coral Tree *Erythrina* **right:** Rose *Rosa*

overleaf: Amaryllis *Amaryllis* **left:** Poinsettia *Euphorbia pulcherrima* **top:** Penstemon *Penstemon*

left: Rose *Rosa* **top:** Zinnia *Zinnia*

Despite all our impressions of flowers, they exist forever outside of our emotions, unaffected. They are, and nothing more— which, of course, is everything. Rooted in absolute presence, their beauty mirrors their astonishing life force. Met with obstacles like a sidewalk, they will find their quiet way, sprouting up through pavement cracks. Ravished by wind, they yield to the gale. Some flowers, like the protea, will

release their seeds for future growth only if a forest fire burns away their protective casings. Laden with raindrops, blossoms bow toward the earth. In blistering sun, they open wider, holding moisture deep in their roots. The spectacular resiliency of a flower in full bloom is contagious. Perhaps this is their greatest seduction, that which sends us

left: Tulip *Tulipa*

rushing headlong into the fields again and
again: that we, too, might reach deep
down into the loamy soil of our time here
and open, open.

Ornamental Kale *Brassica*

Hydrangea *Hydrangea macrophylla*

top: Zinnia *Zinnia* **right:** Hellebore *Helleborus*

left: Pansy *Viola* **top:** Honeywort *Cerinthe*

overleaf: Hydrangea *Hydrangea macrophylla* **top:** Clematis *Clematis*

African Lily *Agapanthus*

left: Pansy *Viola* **top:** Wisteria *Wisteria*

top: African Lily *Agapanthus* **right:** Pansy *Viola*

left: Hydrangea *Hydrangea macrophylla* **top:** Primrose *Primula*

left: Pansy *Viola* **top:** Delphinium *Delphinium*

top: Delphinium *Delphinium* **right:** Grape Hyacinth *Muscari*

left: Siberian Bugloss *Brunnera macrophylla* **top:** Blue Lace Flower *Trachymene coerulea*

left: Hyacinth *Hyacinthus* **top:** Blue Marguerite *Felicia amelloides*

left: Cineraria *Cineraria* **top:** Blue Cowslip *Pulmonaria angustifolia*

Index of Flowers

Daisy
Osteospermum. Perennial. Prefers mild climate, sunny position with light, well-drained soil. Zones 9–11.

Camellia
Camellia japonica. Evergreen shrub/tree. Prefers moist, well-drained soil, moderate winters. Zones 7–8.

Gardenia
Gardenia. Evergreen shrub. Sun- and shade-tolerant; prefers well-drained, humus-rich soil. Zones 9–11.

Alpine Violet
Cyclamen. Perennial. Prefers light, fibrous soil in sun or dappled shade. Zones 7–10.

Hydrangea
Hydrangea macrophylla. Deciduous shrub. Prefers moist, well-drained soil in sun or partial shade. Zones 6–9.

Moth Orchid *Phalaenopsis.* Indoor plant. Prefers high humidity, filtered light, and regular misting. Water weekly in winter.

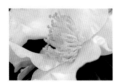

Camellia
Camellia. Evergreen shrub. Prefers moist, well-drained soil, moderate winters. Zones 7–8.

Oriental Lily
Lilium. Perennial bulb. Flowers best with sun for at least half the day and moist, well-drained soil. Zones 6–10.

Mexican Aster
Cosmos. Annual or perennial depending on conditions. Prefers sunny location with well-drained soil. Zones 8–11.

Magnolia
Magnolia grandiflora. Evergreen tree. Requires deep, well-drained soil. Zones 6–11.

Index of Flowers

Gerbera Daisy
Gerbera. Perennial. Needs full sun to partial shade in hot areas with well-drained soil. Zones 8–11.

Dahlia
Dahlia. Perennial. Prefers sunny, sheltered position with well-fertilized soil. Zones 8–10.

Tulip
Tulipa. Perennial bulb. Requires dry, warm summers but cold winters, preferably wet climates, and moist, well-drained soil. Zones 5–9.

Daisy
Leucanthemum maximum. Perennial. Grows in moderately fertile, moist soil in full sun or partial shade. Zones 3–10.

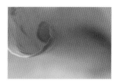

Calla Lily
Zantedeschia. Perennial. Mostly intolerant to dry conditions; prefers full sun or partial shade and well-drained soil. Zones 8–11.

Chrysanthemum.
Chrysanthemum. Perennial. Thrives in sunny location with light, well-drained soil. Zones 4–9.

Hellebore
Helleborus. Perennial or evergreen. Prefers part shade and moist, well-drained soil. Zones 6–10.

Coneflower
Rudbeckia. Perennial. Prefers loamy, moisture-retentive soil in full sun or partial shade. Zones 3–10.

Anthurium
Anthurium. Evergreen shrub or climbing epiphyte depending on conditions. Grows best in tropical climate or greenhouse. Zones 11–12.

Gladiola
Gladiolus. Perennial, cormous. Prefers well-drained, sandy soil in sunny position. Zones 8–11.

Index of Flowers

Hellebore

Helleborus. Perennial or evergreen. Prefers part-shade and moist, well-drained soil. Zones 6–10.

Oxalis

Oxalis. Perennial. Prefers sunny or partly shady location with mulched, well-drained soil and moderate watering. Zones 6–11.

Poppy

Papaver rhoeas. Annual. Frost-hardy; prefers little or no shade and moist soil. Zones 5–9.

Lupine

Lupinus. Annual, perennial, or evergreen shrub depending on conditions. Prefers cool, wet winters and long, dry summers. Plant in full sun with well-drained soil. Zones 7–11.

Orchid

Phalaenopsis. Indoor plant. Prefers high humidity, filtered light, regular misting. Water weekly in winter.

Begonia

Begonia. Tender perennial. Prefers moist, well-drained soil in shady location. Zones 10–11.

Golden Trumpet Tree

Tabebuia. Prefers hot to warm frost-free climate and moist, well-drained soil. Zones 11–12.

Daffodil

Narcissus. Perennial bulb. Grows best in cool conditions, prefers full sun in cool areas, some shade in warmer areas, and rich, fertile soil. Zones 4–10.

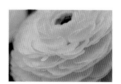

Ranunculus

Ranunculus. Perennial. Grows in moist conditions and sunny or shady locations. Zones 6–10.

Orchid

Cymbidium. Epiphyte or terrestrial. Cool-growing orchid. Potted, prefers bright, filtered light and good ventilation. Water moderately, mist once or twice daily.

Rose
Rosa. Deciduous shrub. Frost-hardy, vigorous plant. Zones 5–11.

Sunflower
Helianthus. Perennial. Prefers bright location, shelter from wind. Zones 4–11.

Tête-à-tête Narcissus
Narcissus. Perennial bulb. Grows best in cool conditions, prefers full sun in cool areas, some shade in warmer areas, and rich, fertile soil. Zones 4–10.

Sunflower
Helianthus. Perennial. Prefers bright location, shelter from wind. Zones 4–11.

Gerbera Daisy
Gerbera. Perennial. Needs full sun to partial shade in hot areas with well-drained soil. Zones 8–11.

Zinnia
Zinnia. Annual. Grows in sunny location in moist, well-drained soil. Moderately frost-hardy. Zones 8–11.

Sunflower
Helianthus. Perennial. Prefers bright location, shelter from wind. Zones 4–11.

Sunflower
Helianthus. Perennial. Prefers bright location, shelter from wind. Zones 4–11.

Sunflower
Helianthus. Perennial. Prefers bright location, shelter from wind. Zones 4–11.

Poppy
Papaver. Annual. Frost-hardy; prefers little or no shade and moist soil. Zones 5–9.

Index of Flowers

Freesia
Freesia. Perennial. Prefers full sun in fertile soil. Zones 9–10.

Dahlia
Dahlia. Perennial. Prefers sunny, sheltered position in well-drained soil. Zones 8–10.

Orchid
Orchid. Indoor plant. Prefers cooler temperatures and filtered light. Water moderately, mist regularly.

Clivia
Clivia. Grows in well-drained soil in partial shade. Zones 10–11.

Begonia
Begonia. Tender perennial. Prefers moist, well-drained soil in shady location. Zones 10–11.

Flowering Maple/ Indian Maple/ Parlour Maple
Abutilon megapotamicum. Grows in moderately fertile, well-drained soil in full sun. Zones 8–10.

Blood Lily
Scadoxus. Perennial. Prefers moderately fertile soil in full sun or light, dappled shade. Zones 6–10.

California Poppy
Eschscholzia californica. Annual. Grows in poor, well-drained soil in full sun. Zones 8–9.

Dahlia
Dahlia. Perennial. Prefers sunny, sheltered position in well-drained soil. Zones 8–10.

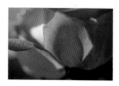

Rose
Rosa. Deciduous shrub. Frost-hardy, vigorous plant. Zones 5–11.

Index of Flowers

Calla Lily
Zantedeschia. Perennial. Mostly intolerant to dry conditions; prefers full sun or partial shade and well-drained soil. Zones 8–11.

Blood-Red Trumpet Vine
Distictis buccinatoria. Evergreen/woody climber. Prefers nearly frost-free climates, needs sunny location and moist, well-drained soil. Zones 9–11.

Alpine Violet
Cyclamen. Perennial. Prefers light, fibrous soil in sun or dappled shade. Zones 7–10.

Angel's Trumpet *Brugmansia*. Grows in fertile, well-drained soil in full sun. Zones 9–12.

Alpine Violet
Cyclamen. Perennial. Prefers light, fibrous soil in sun or dappled shade. Zones 7–10.

Orchid
Paphiopedilum. Indoor plant. Prefers cool to intermediate temperatures. Do not mist.

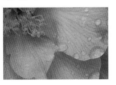

Camellia
Camellia. Evergreen shrub. Prefers moist, well-drained soil, moderate winters. Zones 7–8.

Hibiscus
Hibiscus. Evergreen shrub. Thrives in sun, with slightly acidic, well-drained soil. Zones 7–11.

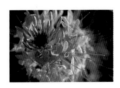

Spider Flower
Cleome. Annual. Requires full sun, regular watering, and shelter from strong winds. Zones 9–11.

Water Lily
Nymphaea. Aquatic perennial. Grows in undisturbed water in full sun. All zones.

Index of Flowers

English Daisy
Bellis perennis. Perennial. Thrives in any good garden soil in sun or partial shade. Zones 3–10.

Crabapple
Malus. Deciduous fruit tree. Frost-hardy; prefers cool climate, full sun, and fertile, loamy soil. Zones 4–9.

Pansy
Viola. Perennial. Prefers full sun or partial shade and moist, well-drained soil. Zones 4–10.

Camellia
Camellia. Evergreen shrub. Prefers moist, well-drained soil, moderate winters. Zones 7–8.

Rockrose
Cistus. Evergreen shrub. Prefers warm, sunny position with well-drained or dry soil. Zones 7–9.

Dahlia
Dahlia. Perennial. Prefers sunny, sheltered position in well-drained soil. Zones 8–10.

Dahlia
Dahlia. Perennial. Prefers sunny, sheltered position in well-drained soil. Zones 8–10.

Aster
Aster. Perennial. Prefers sun and well-drained, compost-enriched soil. Zones 3–9.

Hollyhock
Alcea. Biennial. Frost-hardy; needs shelter from wind; prefers sun, rich, heavy soil, and frequent watering. Zones 4–10.

Dahlia
Dahlia. Perennial. Prefers sunny, sheltered position in well-drained soil. Zones 8–10.

Index of Flowers

**Queensland
Lace Bark**
Brachychiton. Deciduous
tree or shrub. Drought-
resistant; requires well-
drained, preferably acid-
ic soil. Zones 9–12.

Rose
Rosa. Deciduous shrub.
Frost-hardy, vigorous
plant. Zones 5–11.

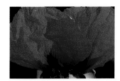

Oriental Poppy
Papaver orientale. Pe-
rennial. Prefers little or
no shade and deep,
moist, well-drained soil.
Zones 3–9.

Salvia
Salvia. Perennial. Grows
in full sun in moist, well-
drained soil. Zones
6–11.

Coral Tree
Erythrina. Deciduous
shrub. Enjoys full sun
and well-drained soil.
Zones 9–11.

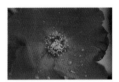

Rose
Rosa. Deciduous shrub.
Frost-hardy, vigorous
plant. Zones 5–11.

Amaryllis
Amaryllis. Perennial.
Grows in moderately
fertile soil in full sun or
partial shade. Zones
8–11.

Poinsettia
Euphorbia pulcherrima.
Prefers very moist, well-
drained soil and bright,
indirect light. Thrives in
warm climates or as
indoor plant. Zone 9.

Penstemon
Penstemon. Perennial.
Very frost-hardy; prefers
fertile soil and full sun.
Zones 6–10.

Rose
Rosa. Deciduous shrub.
Frost-hardy, vigorous
plant. Zones 5–11.

Index of Flowers

Zinnia
Zinnia. Annual. Grows in sunny location in moist, well-drained soil. Moderately frost-hardy. Zones 8–11.

Rose
Rosa. Deciduous shrub. Frost-hardy, vigorous plant. Zones 5–11.

Orchid
Cymbidium. Epiphyte or terrestrial. Cool-growing orchid. Potted, prefers bright, filtered light and good ventilation. Water moderately, mist once or twice daily.

Tulip
Tulipa. Perennial bulb. Requires dry, warm summers but cold winters, preferably wet climates, and moist, well-drained soil. Zones 5–9.

Orchid
Paphiopedilum. Indoor plant. Prefers cool to intermediate temperatures. Do not mist.

Ornamental Kale
Brassica. Biennial. Prefers lime-rich, moist soil in sheltered, sunny location. Zones 7–11.

Hydrangea
Hydrangea macrophylla. Deciduous shrub. Prefers moist, well-drained soil in sun or partial shade. Zones 6–9.

Zinnia
Zinnia. Annual. Grows in sunny location in moist, well-drained soil. Moderately frost-hardy. Zones 8–11.

Hellebore
Helleborus. Perennial or evergreen. Prefers part-shade and moist, well-drained soil. Zones 6–10.

Pansy
Viola. Perennial. Grows in full sun but appreciates shelter from drying winds. Zones 4–10.

Index of Flowers

Honeywort
Cerinthe. Annual. Grows in part shade or full sun if in a sheltered spot. Zones 7–10.

Hydrangea
Hydrangea macrophylla. Deciduous shrub. Prefers moist, well-drained soil in sun or partial shade. Zones 6–9.

Clematis
Clematis. Woody climber. Prefers well-drained, humus-rich, permanently cool soil with good moisture retention. Zones 5–9.

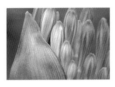

African Lily
Agapanthus. Prefers full sun; will grow in any soil as long as it gets water in spring and summer. Zones 9–11.

Pansy
Viola. Perennial. Grows in full sun but appreciates shelter from drying winds. Zones 4–10.

Wisteria
Wisteria. Deciduous climber. Prefers sunny position and humus-rich soil. Zones 5–10.

African Lily
Agapanthus. Prefers full sun; will grow in any soil as long as it gets water in spring and summer. Zones 9–11.

Pansy
Viola. Perennial. Grows in full sun but appreciates shelter from drying winds. Zones 4–10

Hydrangea
Hydrangea macrophylla. Deciduous shrub. Prefers moist, well-drained soil in sun or partial shade. Zones 6–9.

Primrose
Primula. Perennial. Prefers part shade, ample water, and fertile, well-drained soil. Zones 5–9.

Index of Flowers

Pansy
Viola. Perennial. Grows in full sun but appreciates shelter from drying winds. Zones 4–10.

Delphinium
Delphinium. Annual. Prefers full sun with shelter from strong winds and well-drained soil. Zones 3–9.

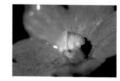

Delphinium
Delphinium. Annual. Prefers full sun with shelter from strong winds and well-drained soil. Zones 3–9.

Grape Hyacinth *Muscari*. Perennial. Prefers cool areas and rich, well-drained soil. Zones 4–10.

Siberian Bugloss
Brunnera macrophylla. Perennial. Prefers humus-rich soil with leafy mulch and a position in dappled shade. Zones 3–9.

Blue Lace Flower *Trachymene coerulea*. Annual. Prefers a sunny location with moist, well-drained soil. Zones 9–12.

Hyacinth
Hyacinthus. Perennial bulb. Prefers full sun in marginal climates, where some shade keeps the bulbs cool. Zones 5–9.

Blue Marguerite
Felicia amelloides. Evergreen subshrub. Frost-tender; requires full sun and well-drained, gravelly soil. Zones 9–11.

Cineraria
Cineraria. Perennial/subshrub. Prefers humus-rich soil and plenty of sun. Zones 9–11.

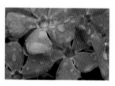

Blue Cowslip
Pulmonaria angustifolia. Perennial. Prefers cool, moist soil in light shade. Zones 3–9.